I Jus   e

....

Replacing Suicidal Thoughts with Hope

David Powlison

New
Growth
Press

www.newgrowthpress.com

New Growth Press, Greensboro, NC 27404
Copyright © 2010 by Christian Counseling & Educational Foundation
All rights reserved. Published 2010.

Cover Design: Tandem Creative, Tom Temple, tandemcreative.net
Typesetting: Robin Black, www.blackbirdcreative.biz

ISBN-10: 1-935273-70-1
ISBN-13: 978-1-935273-70-7

Library of Congress Cataloging-in-Publication Data

Powlison, David, 1949-
  I just want to die : replacing suicidal thoughts with hope / David Powlison.
    p. cm.
  Includes bibliographical references.
  ISBN-13: 978-1-935273-70-7 (alk. paper)
  ISBN-10: 1-935273-70-1 (alk. paper)
  1. Depression, Mental—Religious aspects—Christianity.
2. Suicide—Religious aspects—Christianity. 3. Hope—
Religious aspects—Christianity. I. Title.
  BV4910.34.P69 2010
  248.8'625—dc22
                                        2010023094
Printed in South Korea

25 24 23 22 21 20 19   11 12 13 14 15

Are you having suicidal thoughts and feelings? Perhaps you are convinced that life is not worth living. You feel like your world is collapsing in on you. Your life seems hopeless—like a black hole with all love, hope, and joy sucked out. If you are contemplating suicide, you have already done a lot of thinking about your life. But have you also thought about how God views your life?

Your Life Matters to God

Right now you are living in a world of despair. You can't see any solution to your problems. You're not looking forward to anything. The future seems empty.

But God's perspective on your life is very different. Your life is precious to him. He knows everything about you—even how many hairs are on your head. He loves you to such a degree that he sent his own Son to die for you (John 3:16).Your life is so significant to him that he forbids you to take it. God says that all murder is wrong, and that includes the self-murder of suicide (Exodus 20:13).

Your Life Matters to Other People

Perhaps you've been thinking about how long you have been depressed and sad. Are you feeling like a burden to other people? Even though they don't say it, do you feel like everyone would be better off without you?

The way you are thinking is tragically wrong. It's a lie that anyone—neighbors, parents, children, spouse, friends, coworkers, nurses, or mere acquaintances—would ever be helped by your suicide. Someone else's suicide is disturbing and unsettling. Those you leave behind will *not* be relieved. Instead, they will be left with terrible burdens. What are those burdens?

First, those who know you and care about you will never understand why. They will ask the same questions over and over again: "Why did you to do this? Why did you leave us? Why didn't you ask for help? Why weren't we able to help you?" The "why" questions will haunt those you leave behind.

Second, they will feel guilt. Added to the heartache of losing you will be the heartache of feeling responsible. They will wonder if your suicide was a response to something that they did or didn't do. They will be left with a feeling of overwhelming, personal failure.

Third, those you leave behind won't think you did them a favor with your suicide; instead, they will feel as if you didn't love them. How could you have loved them *and* hurt them so badly? Suicide is a selfish act. It cuts off a relationship, and leaves no hope for reconciliation. Those you leave behind will feel a very deep emptiness.

Fourth, suicide models the choice to run away, as if killing yourself is the way to solve life's problems. Suicide says that the way to deal with guilt, failure, disappointment, and hardship is to take your own life. That model has a powerful negative influence. So rather than leaving those around you better off, you are actually leaving them a role model that could negatively impact how they handle their own struggles.

Consider What Is True

Suicidal thinking is full of falsehoods. It can be hard for you, as you struggle, to recognize the lies. So stick to a few simple truths about God and you. Remind yourself of them every time you start thinking that suicide is a good solution to your problems.

1. In love, God has come in person as a Savior from death:

   But now, this is what the LORD says—
   he who created you, O Jacob,
   he who formed you, O Israel:
   "Fear not, for I have redeemed you;
   I have summoned you by name; you are mine."
   (Isaiah 43:1)

   But God demonstrates his own love for us in this: While we were still sinners, Christ died for us. (Romans 5:8)

2. God says that suicide is wrong because you are taking a life.

   You shall not murder. (Exodus 20:13).

3. When you pour out your heart to God, he will hear you:

   In my alarm I said,
   "I am cut off from your sight!"

Yet you heard my cry for mercy
   when I called to you for help. (Psalm 31:22)

Evening, morning and noon
   I cry out in distress,
   and he hears my voice. (Psalm 55:17)

Bring Your Hopelessness to the One Who Is True

Your Savior is not surprised or put off by your hope-less feelings. He wants you to bring your despair to him and cry for help right now, in the middle of your darkness and pain. Throughout history God's children have cried to him. He has helped them. Psalm 86 captures for us how David cried out his despair to God thousands of years ago: "In the day of my trouble I will call to you, for you will answer me" (v. 7).

Today is your day of trouble. Tell Jesus all your sorrows, all your troubles, and all the reasons suicide is on your mind. Do you feel, like David, that you are in the "depths of the grave" (v. 13)? Say out loud to God, "Hear my prayer, O Lord; Listen to my cry for mercy"

(v. 6). On this day the living God promises to listen to you and help you. "You will seek me and find me when you seek me with all your heart" (Jeremiah 29:13).

Your Reasons for Despair—God's Reasons for Hope

Why are you feeling hopeless? Are you struggling with physical suffering? A broken relationship? Shame and guilt from mistakes and failures? An unrealized dream? What problem do you believe suicide will solve?

Your suicidal feelings and actions don't come out of the blue. They have reasons you can discover and understand. Your particular reasons will show you how you're experiencing, interpreting, and reacting to your world. When you discover your reasons, you will also describe what is most important to you. The loss or pain that makes you feel like your life is not worth living points to the thing that you believe would make your life worth living.

We will look at four different reasons for hopelessness. As you read, look for the specific reasons you are feeling hopeless. Then discover the hope that God brings to you in your *particular* troubles.

Unrelenting Suffering. Your hopelessness might stem from overwhelming suffering. The death of someone close to you, your own chronic pain and illness, postpartum depression, a broken relationship, poverty, racial prejudice, etc. are all situations that can fill you with despair.

If this is why you feel hopeless, read through Psalm 31. This psalm, written by David, vividly captures the feeling of wasting away with grief. These words were on Jesus' heart and lips as he was dying.

> Be merciful to me, O LORD, for I am in distress;
> my eyes grow weak with sorrow, my soul and my
> body with grief. My life is consumed by anguish
> and my years by groaning. (vv. 9–10)

Is this what your life is like?

This psalm is also filled with hope. David remembers that God sees him in his affliction and knows all about his troubles. He remembers that in God's presence he is safe.

> How great is your goodness, which you have
> stored up for those who fear you, which you

bestow in the sight of men on those who take
refuge in you. In the shelter of your presence
you hide them from the intrigues of men; in
your dwelling you keep them safe from accusing
tongues. (vv. 19–20)

David's life, like yours, is full of troubles and dis-
couragement. Yet because God is with him, he has
hope. He says, "You heard my cry for mercy when I
called to you for help" (v. 22). And he ends with this
call: "Be strong and take heart, all you who hope in
the LORD" (v. 24). David is able to endure with cour-
age because God is with him.

God is calling you to persevere in your suffering, but not by simply gritting your teeth. Persevering
through suffering is only possible when you put your
hope in the living God. He promises to come near
to you, to be present with you, and to let you experience his goodness right in the middle of your pain
and difficulty. Jesus was able to persevere through the
greatest time of suffering that any human has ever
endured. He did this "for the joy set before him" of
doing his Father's will and of bringing salvation to his

people (Hebrews 12:2). As you fix your eyes on Jesus, the author and perfecter of your faith, you too will be able to persevere through this time of suffering and find joy in living for God.

Personal Failure. Your suicidal thoughts and feelings might be related to your failures. Is your hopelessness an attempt to atone for your sins, to punish yourself, to avoid feelings of shame? Perhaps you feel so full of guilt and shame that you don't want to be around people or even continue to live. Can you find hope when you've blown it so badly that you think you will never be able to hold your head up again?

One amazing thing about the Bible is that it is full of real people who made serious missteps—just like you. David wrote Psalm 32 after he committed adultery, the woman became pregnant, and (to cover up things) he arranged to have the woman's husband murdered. You can read the whole story in 2 Samuel 11–12.

In Psalm 32 he vividly describes his experience of despair. Perhaps you are also feeling like this:

> My bones wasted away through my groaning
> all day long. For day and night your hand was

heavy upon me; my strength was sapped as in
the heat of summer. (vv. 3–4)

David's experience of guilt and failure comes
partly from God and partly from his own conscience.
But why is this psalm also full of joy, instead of only
despair and shame? It is because of what God does for
David in the midst of his nightmare of guilt. His joy
comes from God's forgiveness of him and from God's
promise to guide him (Psalm 31:1–2, 8).

Here's someone, like you, who is living with terrible personal failure. But instead of meditating on his
failures, instead of turning his sins over and over in
his mind, he chooses to remember who God is. He
knows the God who forgives. He trusts the God who
promises to keep his eyes on him, who will personally
instruct, lead, and counsel. So he ends like this: "The
LORD's unfailing love surrounds the man who trusts
in him"; and he adds a call to joy: "Rejoice in the
LORD and be glad, you righteous; sing, all you who
are upright in heart!" (Psalm 32:10–11).

What an amazing turnaround! Someone who
knows his sinfulness, but also knows God's mercy,

can be called righteous by the grace and mercy of God. You, too, can experience what David experienced. But to do so, you must seek this Lord. David describes how he felt after his sin was exposed, when he hadn't yet confessed his sins to God. His vitality drains away; he feels hopeless and lifeless. If that is you, then do what David did—go to God with your sins and failures. Your Savior is who he says he is: merciful. He does what he says he does: he forgives. Turn from self-absorbed misery and find freely-given mercies.

Here is a wonderful description of seeking God in the midst of guilt: David says, "I acknowledged my sin to you and did not cover up my iniquity. I said, 'I will confess my transgressions to the Lord'—and you forgave the guilt of my sin" (Psalm 32:5). Notice that David is turning to God about his failures. He is not turning inward. He is not turning to those around him. He doesn't live in shame anymore. He is forgiven. He can hold up his head and write about it in the Bible, recording his sins for all time. This is because he knows that God is with him.

And then David gives the key to having God with him: "Therefore let everyone who is godly pray to you" (Psalm 32:6). He knows that asking for help brings him into God's presence where he is safe from trouble—even the trouble he brought upon himself.

Failed Dreams. You can also struggle with hopelessness when the thing that has given your life meaning is taken from you. Perhaps it's a job you didn't get, an unrealized life goal, or your children turning out a certain way. Whatever you have organized your life around, its absence will leave you feeling empty and despairing.

Perhaps you didn't realize how important your dream was to you until it didn't materialize. Now you are experiencing the hopelessness of a failed dream. But what does a failed dream reveal about where you find meaning? When what you have lived for is taken from you, it can feel like you are dying. Life is empty. You feel so much pain or emptiness that suicide seems like your only alternative. But God has a better way. He will give you true, lasting hope that can never be taken away from you.

God says, in Psalm 33, that it is he who "foils the plans of the nations" (v. 10). Later in the psalm he says why: because all those hopes are futile. "No king is saved by the size of his army; no warrior escapes by his great strength. A horse is a vain hope for deliverance; despite all its great strength it cannot save" (vv. 16–17). Now you probably didn't set your hopes on an army and horses (although trust in physical strength and personal abilities is still a common false dream). What you trust in are those things on which you build your life, your identity, your goals, and your success. The details may be different from people thousands of years ago, but the result is the same. Anything you trust in besides God's steadfast love for you is futile.

But Jesus Christ is risen! When you put your hope in God's love, he will deliver your soul from death (vv. 18–19). Anything else comes up empty. Let the death of your dreams be the doorway to putting your trust in God's love for you. He will be your help and shield. As you "trust in his holy name" (v. 21), he will deliver your soul from death, from thoughts of death, and from trying to take your own life.

False hopes. Perhaps your suicidal thinking is not from hopelessness, but from false hopes. Dreaming about and planning your suicide is what brings you hope. You believe that killing yourself will bring about some wonderful answer or solution to your problems. If you have been deeply betrayed and hurt by someone, you might see suicide as a way to make others suffer.

You might hope that suicide will bring an end to your suffering, and that those you love will be better off without you. Or you might hope that your suicidal gesture will get you what you want—attention, love, or even a break from the pressures of life. But whatever your hopes are—"I'll be in a place of peace," or "Then everyone will know how much they made me suffer."—if they include suicide as a solution, they are false hopes.

Suicide is *never* an answer. Two wrongs *never* make a right. Don't forget that suicide is a great wrong. If you have been wronged, please don't think that suicide is the way to make that wrong better. God offers you true, living hope, not a false hope based on your death. Hope from God comes in the midst of evil and trouble, and it is a hope that will never end.

Paul talks about true and living hope in the second half of Romans 8. True hope comes from knowing God as your Father and receiving his Spirit as a gift. Living as a child of God means that instead of responding to trouble by hurting yourself, you go to your heavenly Father for help. He gives you his Spirit to help you in your weakness and even teach you how and what to ask for (vv. 15–16). The Spirit of God will teach you that your "present sufferings are not worth comparing with the glory that will be revealed" in you (v. 18).

We live in a world where bad things happen. Your heavenly Father freely gives the best gift of all—the Spirit of life, the Holy Spirit of Jesus. He gives the gift of a relationship now that will lead to an indestructible life forever. There is nothing in this world that can separate you from God's love—not trouble, distress, hardship, or anything in all creation (v. 35). The love of God in Christ Jesus will keep you safe. It's yours for the asking. All who seek, find.

The Resurrection—Your Reason for Hope

How do you know that the promises God makes to you are true? How do you know that the living God gives true, substantial hope? Because Jesus defeated death. As a willing and sinless substitute, he died in our place on the cross. And God raised him to life and joy. He is alive. Peter explains it this way: "Praise be to the God and Father of our Lord Jesus Christ! In his great mercy he has given us new birth into a living hope through the resurrection of Jesus Christ from the dead, and into an inheritance that can never perish, spoil or fade—kept in heaven for you" (1 Peter 1:3–4). Your Father in heaven has great mercy. He makes us alive. He gives us realistic joy and hope.

Jesus is alive! His resurrection is his guarantee that you can live in real hope. Your hope is not based on a pipe dream that changed circumstances, passing of time, a new set of friends, or ending it all will somehow cure how horrible you feel. He gives living hope based on the physical reality of the resurrection of Jesus Christ. Because the resurrection happened and Jesus is alive, well, and at work, your story can end in life.

Peter goes on to say that along with your hope comes "an inheritance that can never perish, spoil or fade" (v. 4). When you have this living hope, then what you get out of life (your "inheritance") won't be destroyed or ruined by your troubles.

Practical Strategies for Change

It's easy to see the risk factors for suicide—depression, suffering, disillusioning experiences, failure—but there are also ways to get your life back on track by building protective factors into your life.

Ask for Help

How do you get the living hope that God offers you in Jesus? By asking. Jesus said, "Ask and it will be given to you; seek and you will find; knock and the door will be opened to you. For everyone who asks receives; he who seeks finds; and to him who knocks, the door will be opened" (Matthew 7:7–8).

Suicide operates in a world of death, despair, and aloneness. Jesus Christ creates a world of life, hope, and community. Ask God for help, and keep on asking. Don't stop asking. You need him to fill you every day with the hope of the resurrection.

At the same time you are asking God for help, tell other people about your struggle with hopelessness. God uses his people to bring life, light, and hope. Suicide, by definition, happens when someone is all alone. Getting in relationship with wise, caring people will protect you from despair and acting out of despair. Share your struggles with those who love you and ask them to pray for you. God will answer your cries and theirs.

But what if you are bereaved and alone? If you know Jesus, you still have a family—his family is your family. Become part of a community of other Christians. Look for a church where Jesus is at the center of teaching and worship. Get in relationship with people who can help you, but don't stop with just getting help. Find people to love, serve, and give to. Even if your life has been stripped barren by lost relationships, God can and will fill your life with helpful and healing relationships.

Grow in Godly Life Skills

Another protective factor is to grow in godly living. Many of the reasons for despair come from not living a godly, fruitful life. Life becomes empty. You need to learn the skills that make godly living possible. What are some of those skills?

- Conflict resolution. Learn to problem-solve by entering into human difficulties and growing through them. (Read the minibook, *Conflict: A Redemptive Opportunity*)
- Seek and grant forgiveness. Hopeless thinking is often the result of guilt and bitterness. (Read the minibook, *Forgiving Others: Joining Wisdom and Love*)
- Learn to give to others. Suicide is a selfish act. It's a lie that others will be better off without you. Work to replace your faulty thinking by reaching out to others who also are struggling. Take what you have learned in this minibook and pass it on to at least one other person. Whatever hope God gives you, give to someone else who is struggling with despair.

Live for God

When you live for the God who gave his only Son's life for you, you find genuine meaning for your life. This purpose is far bigger than your suffering, your failures, the death of your dreams, and the disillusionment of your hopes. Living by faith in God for his purposes will protect you from suicidal and despairing thoughts. God wants to use your personality, your skills, your life situation, and even your struggle with despair to bring hope to others.

He has already prepared fruitful things for you to do. The apostle Paul says, in the Bible, "For we are God's workmanship, created in Christ Jesus to do good works, which God prepared in advance for us to do" (Ephesians 2:10). As you seek to work good in whatever circumstances you face, wherever God places you, you will find meaning, purpose, and joy. And when the race is over, it will be your Father in heaven who ends your days by calling you home. Until that time, may Jesus himself bless you, keep you, make his heavenly Father's face shine upon you, and give you peace.

Endnotes

1 Timothy S. Lane, *Conflict: A Redemptive Opportunity* (Greensboro, NC: New Growth Press, 2009).
2 Timothy S. Lane, *Forgiving Others: Joining Wisdom and Love* (Greensboro, NC: New Growth Press, 2008).